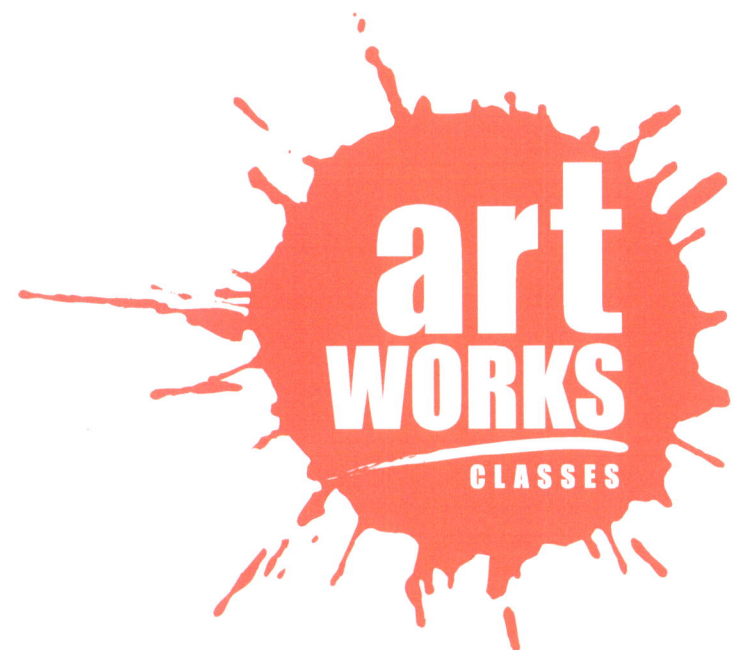

Level 1

Beginners guide to step-drawing

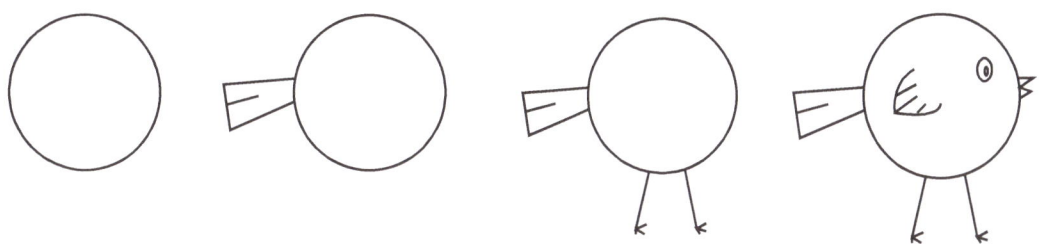

This book belongs to:

NAME _____

DATE _____

Contents

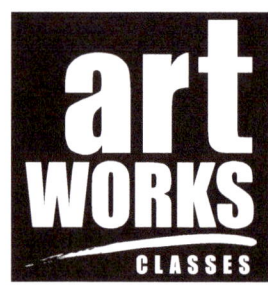

Bethesda
    7740 Old Georgetown Rd
    MD 20814
McLean
    6730 Curran Street
    VA 22101

Instructions

The step drawings on the left page will guide you with your drawings on the right page.

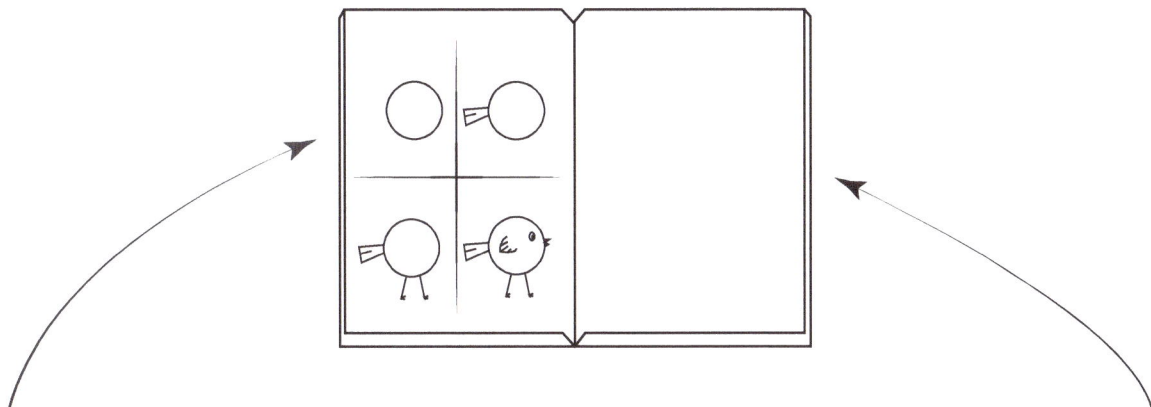

Begin with step one and draw the biggest shapes first. Remember to draw lightly

Dotted lines mean to erase

Continue with remaining steps until picture is completed

Have Fun

Go to www.artworksclasses.com to see video tutorials.

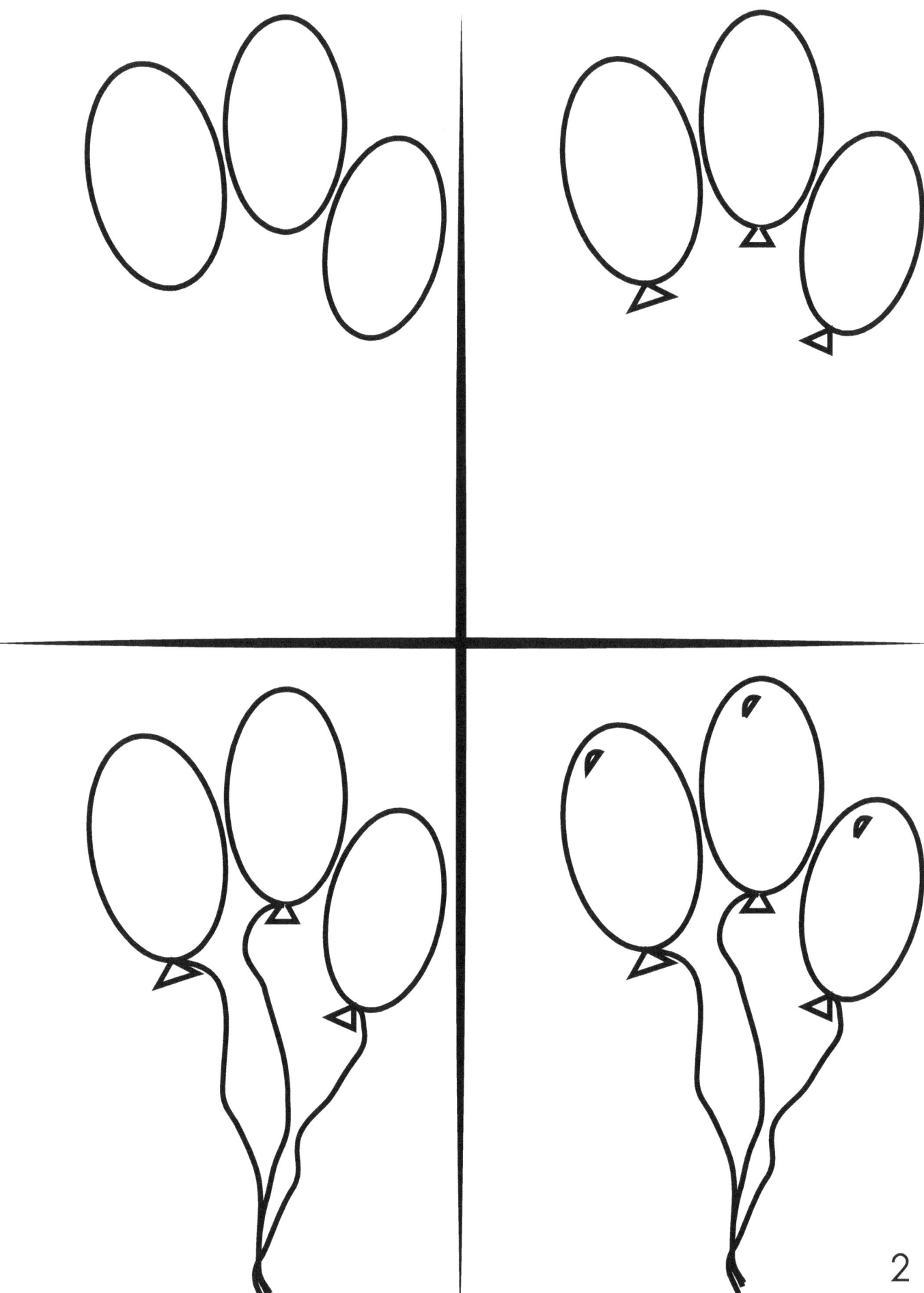

2

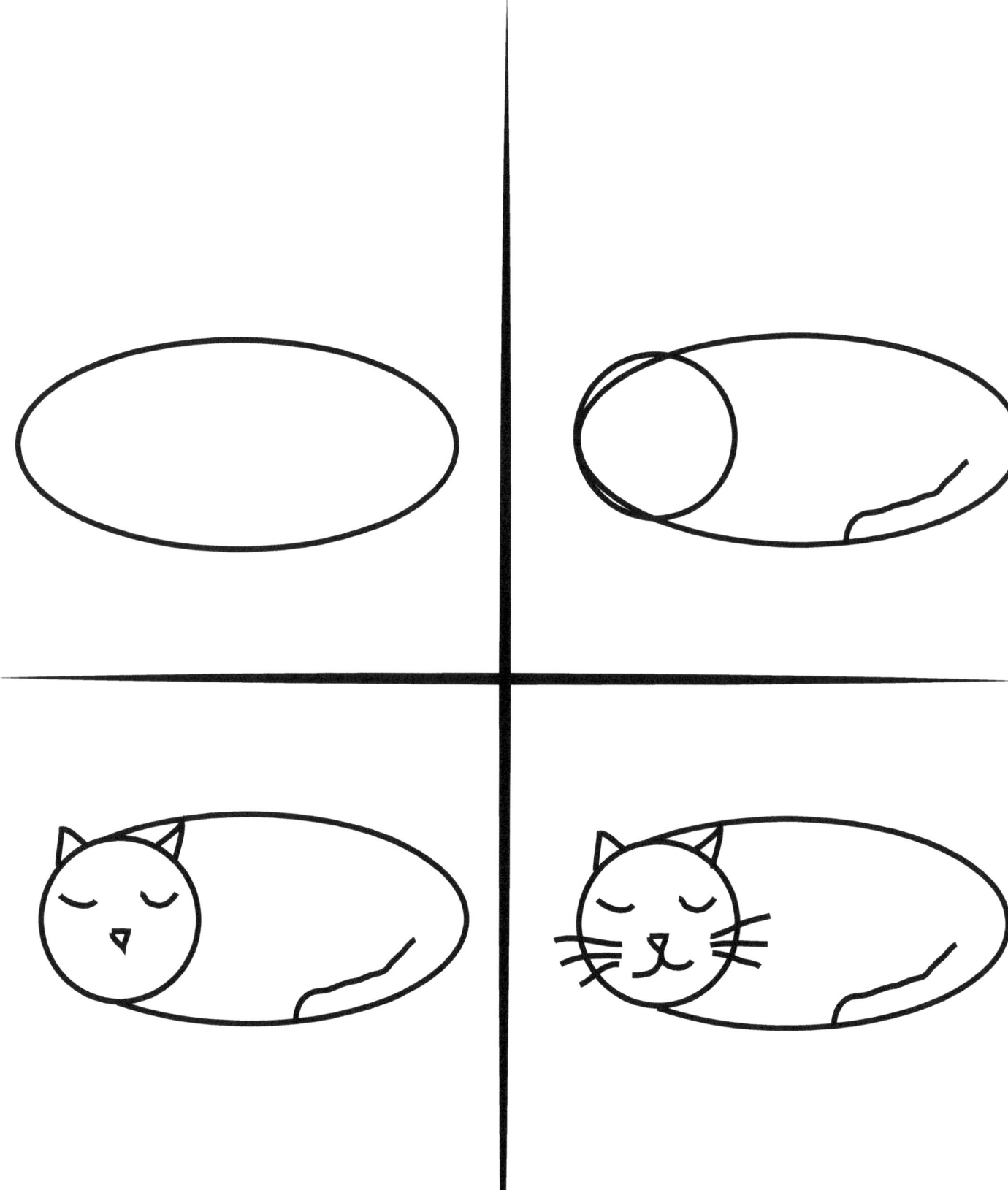

4

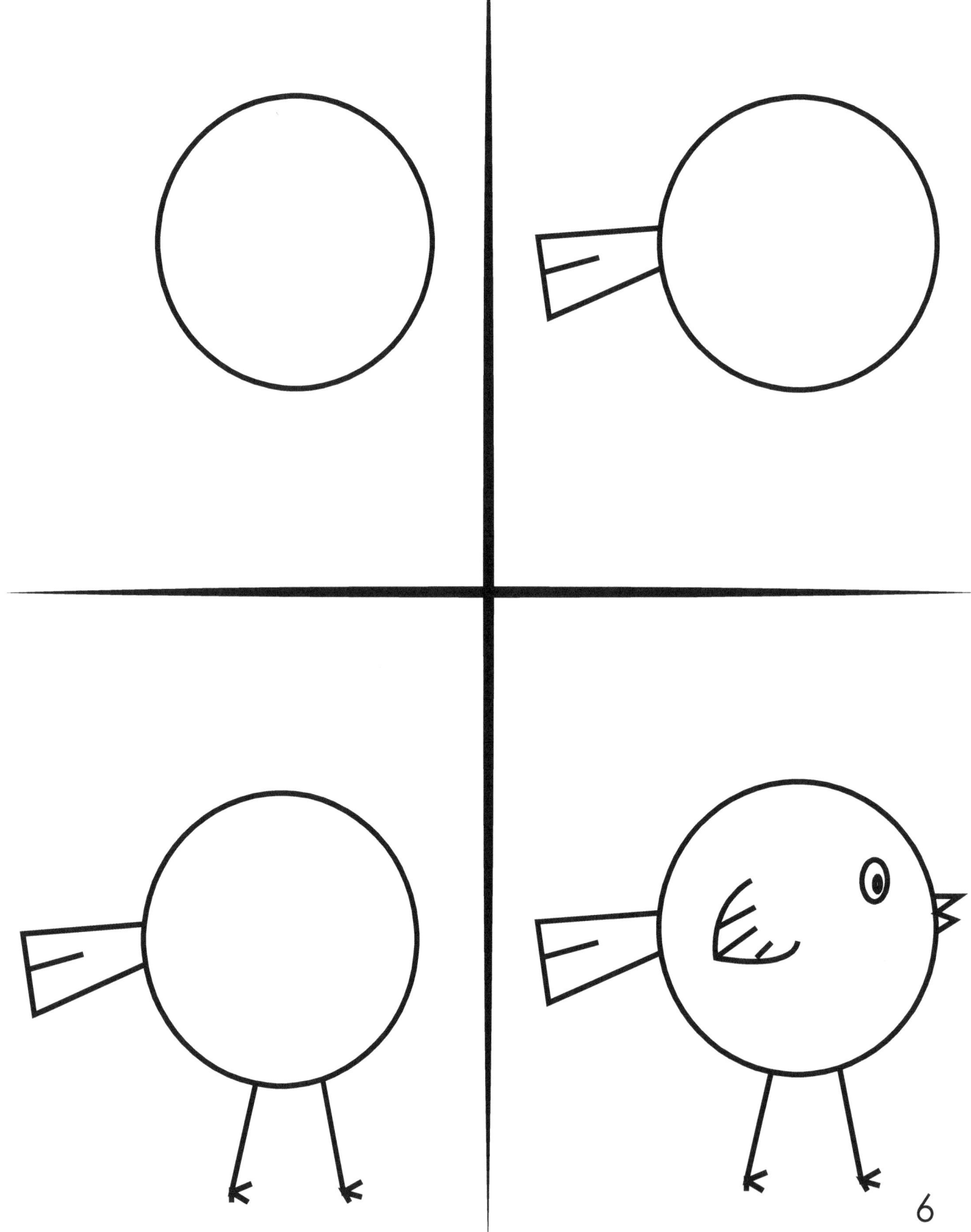

6

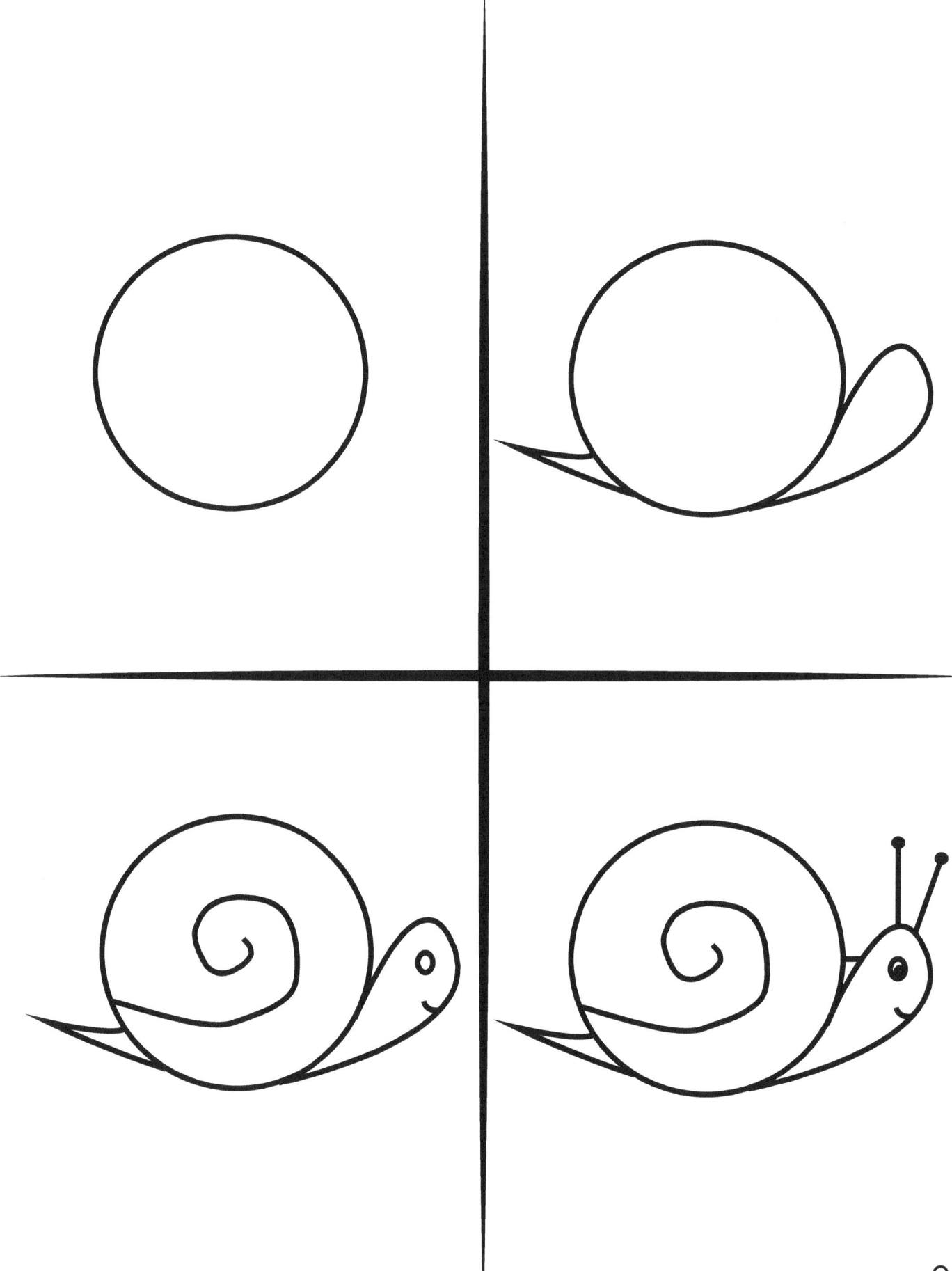

8

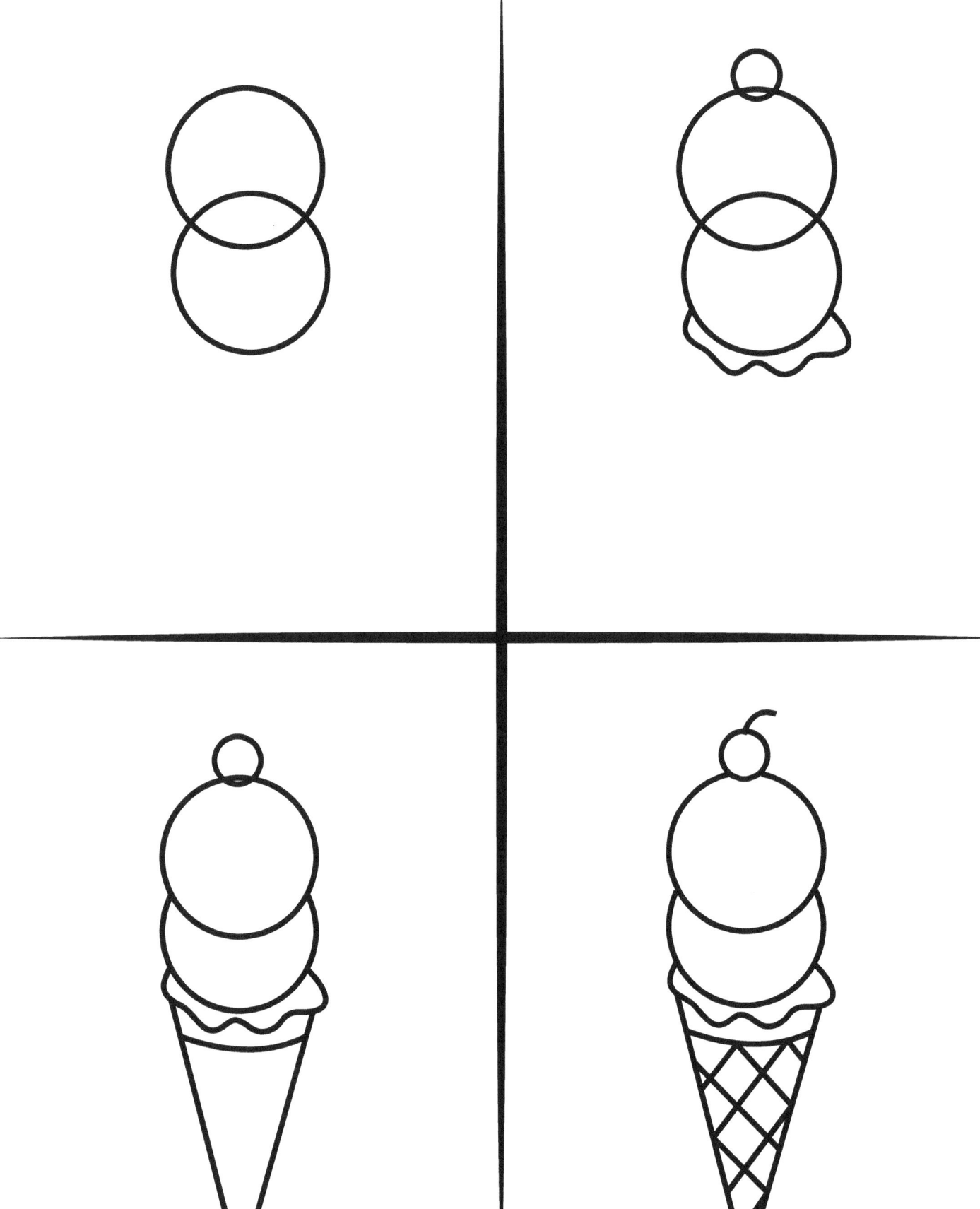

10

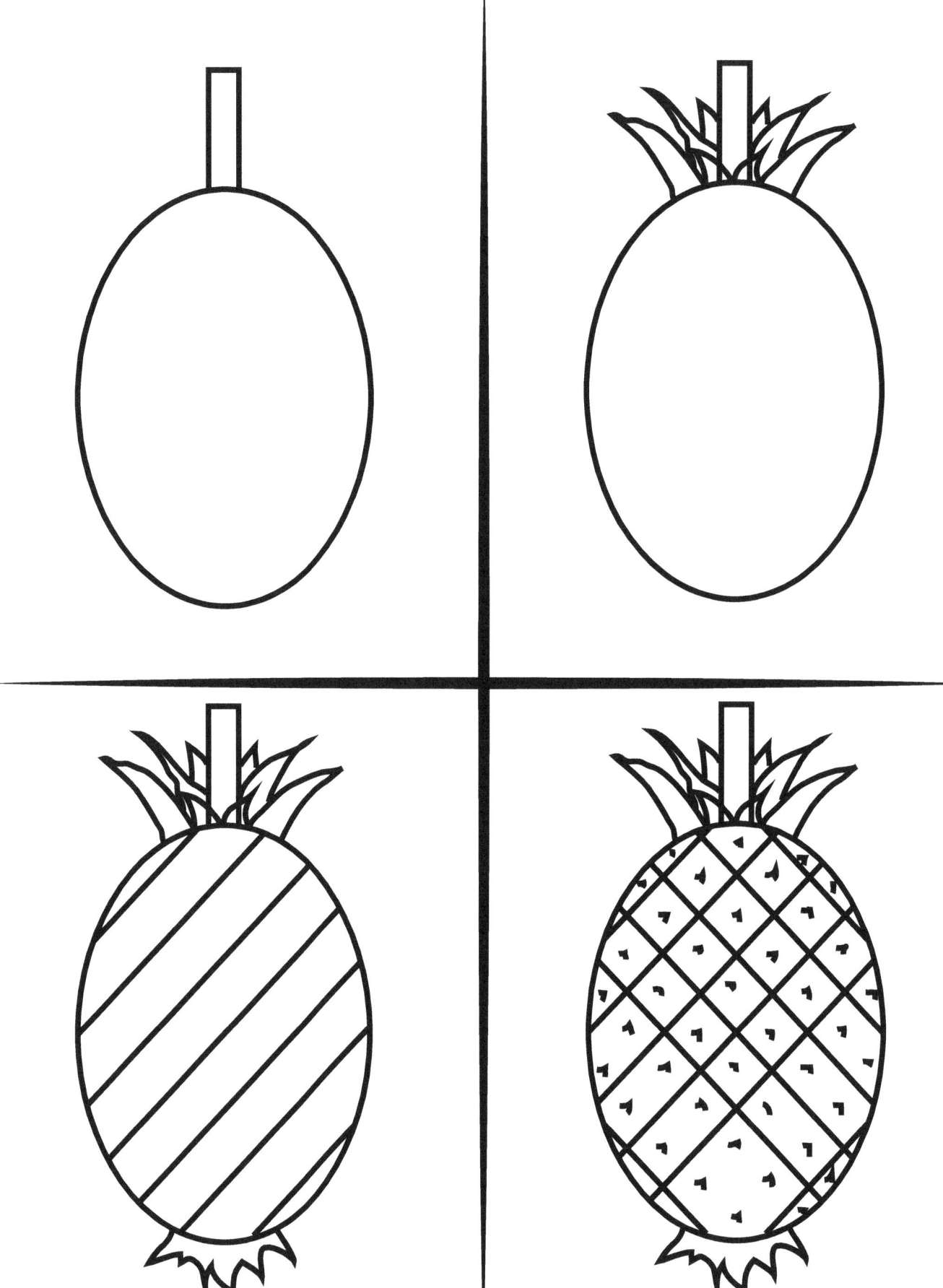

12

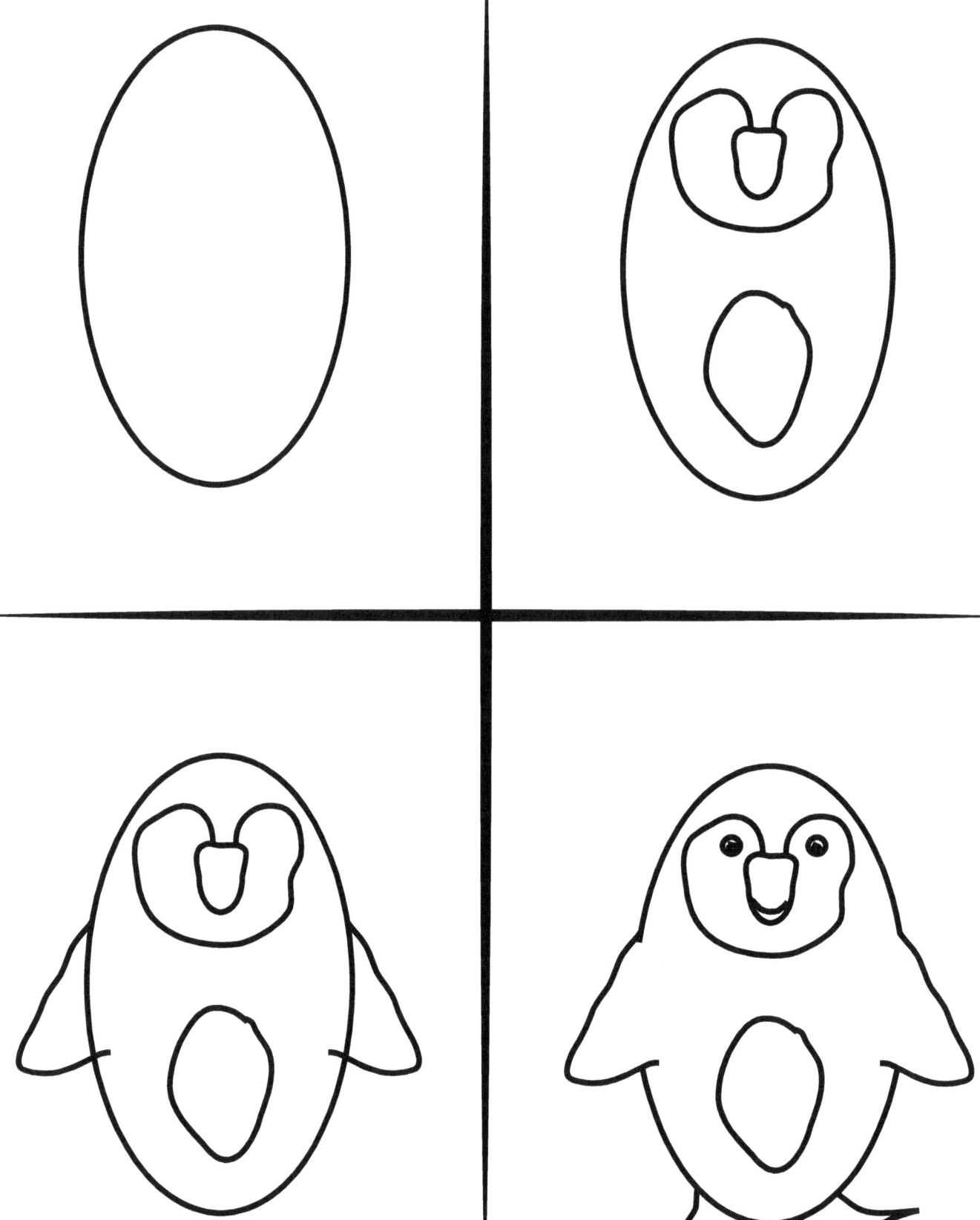

14

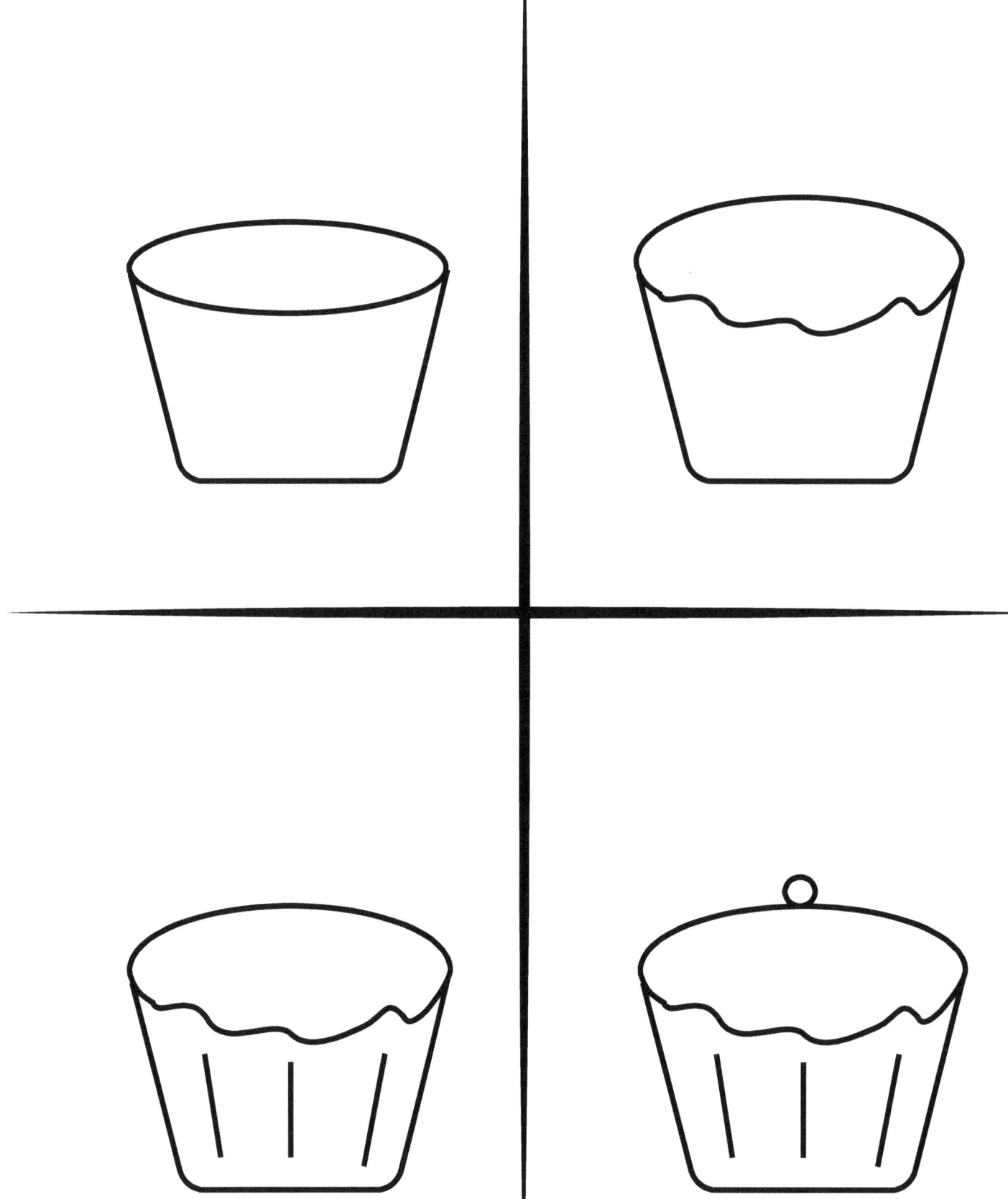

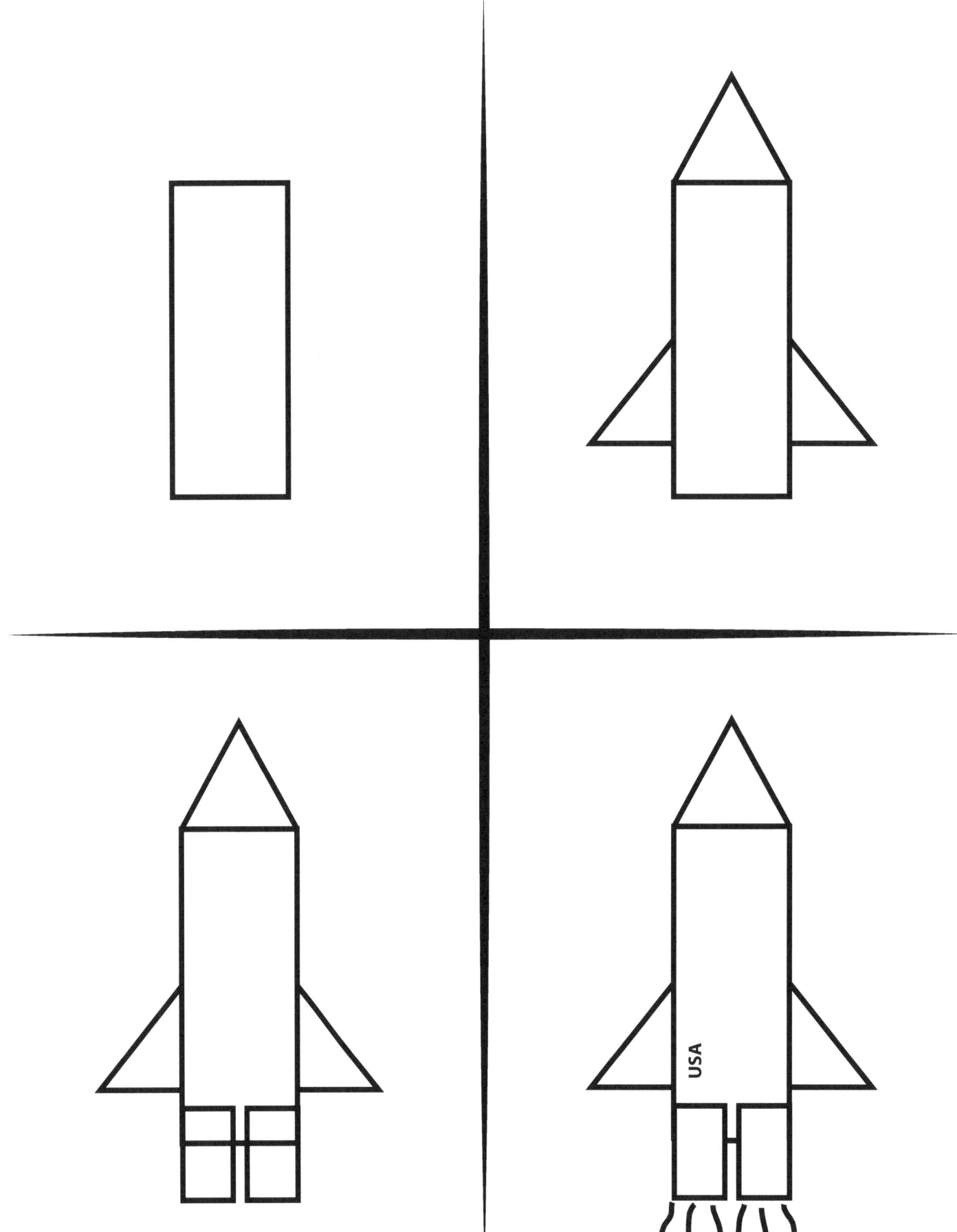

18

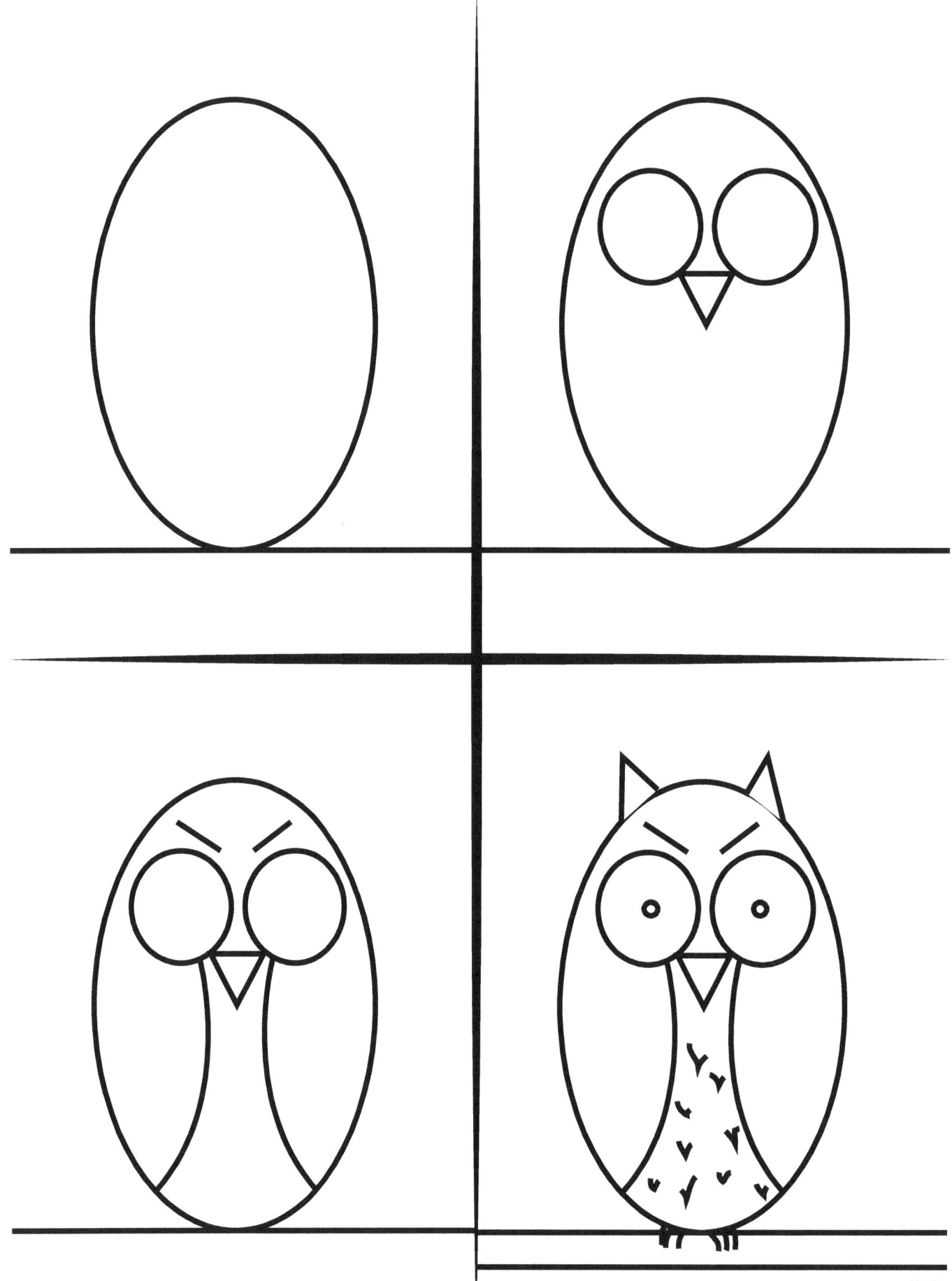

20

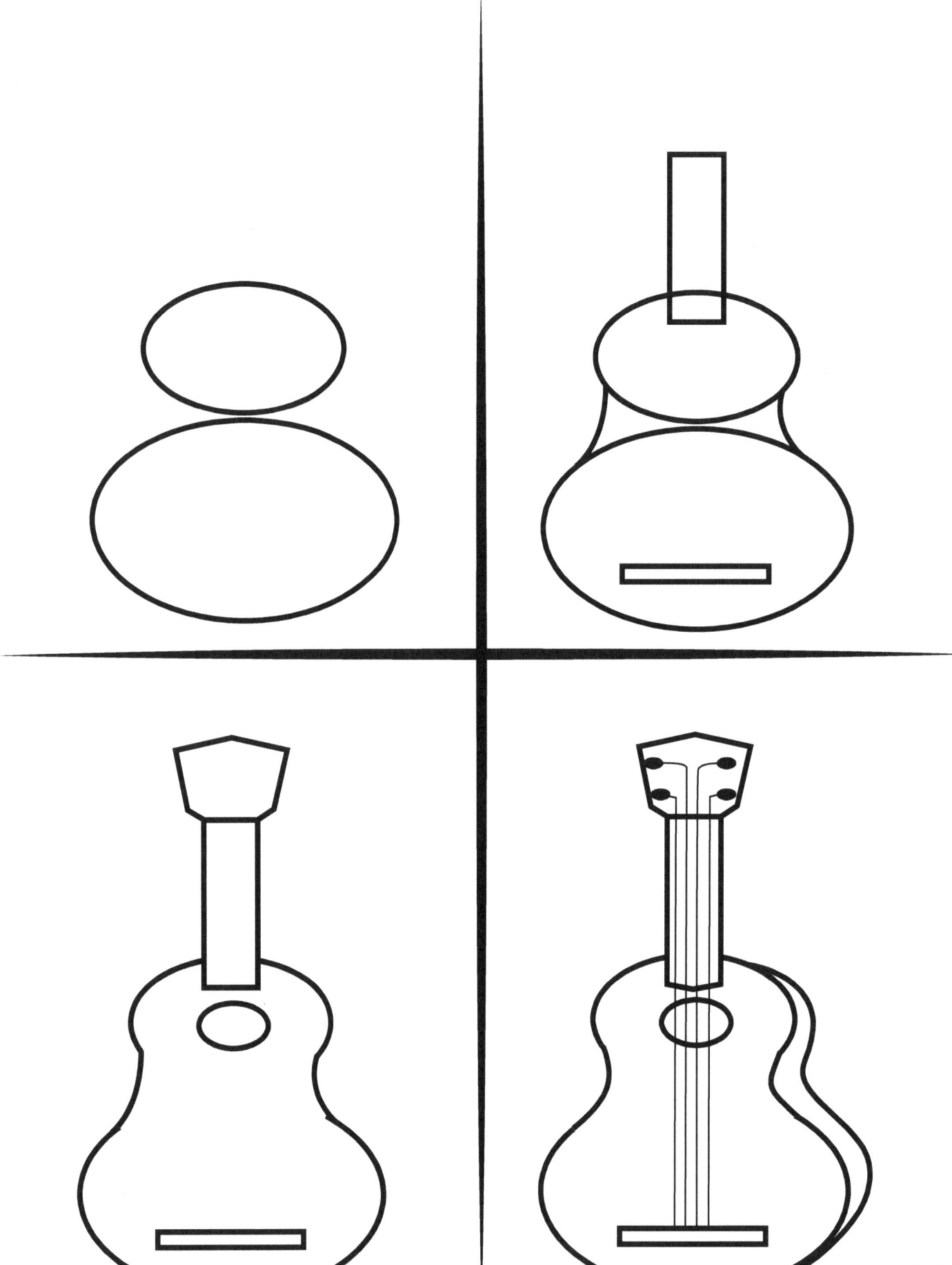

22

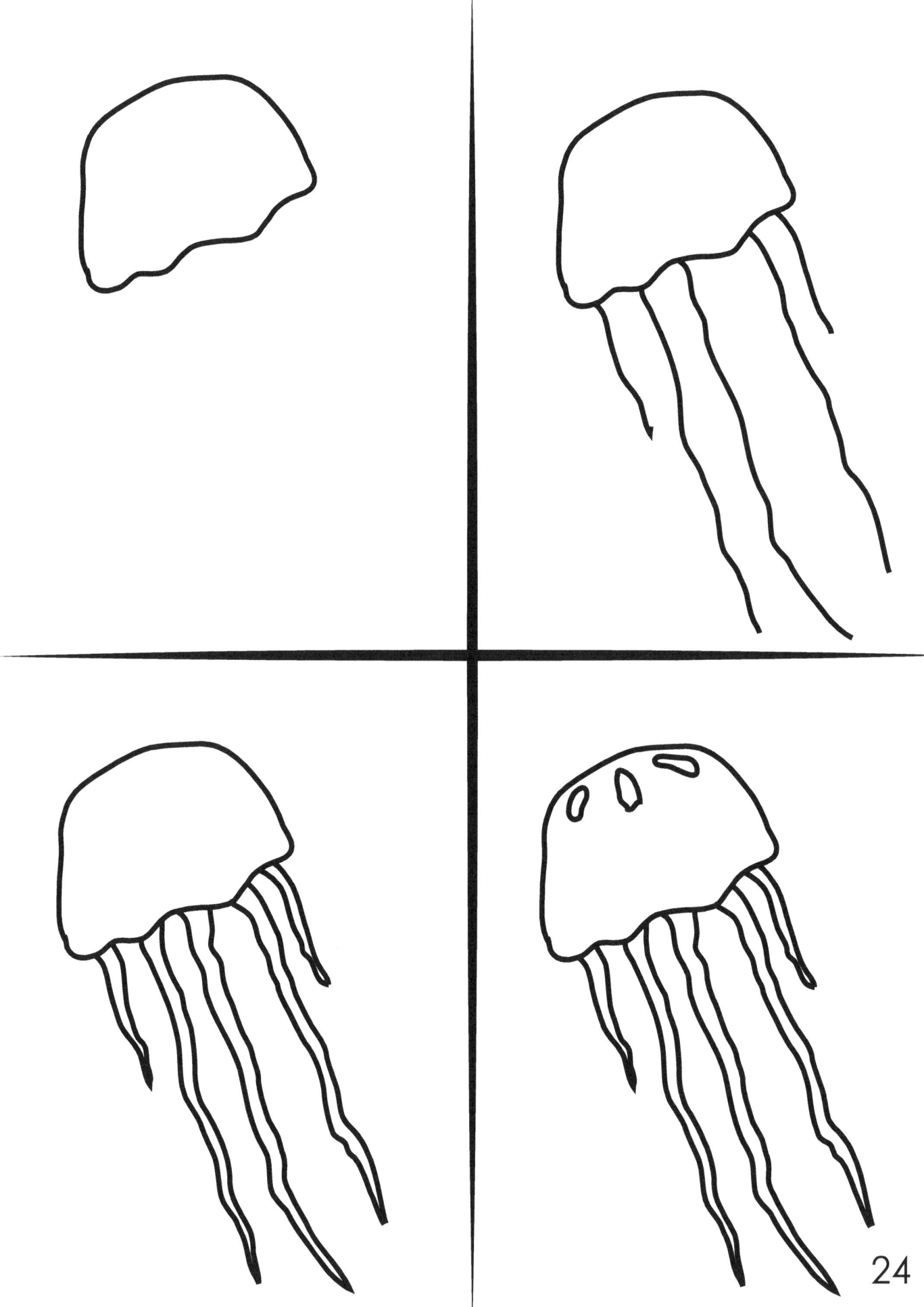

24

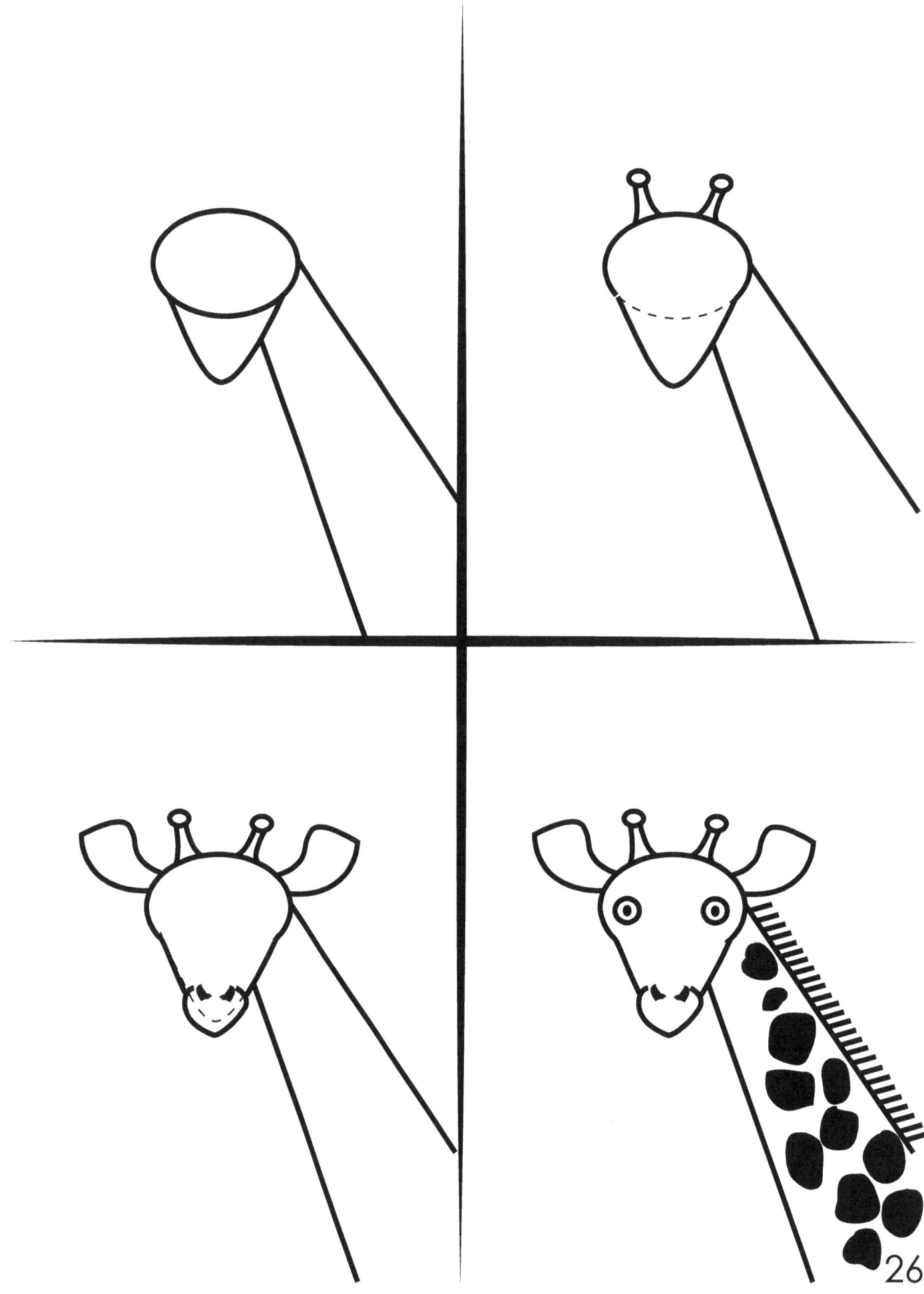

26

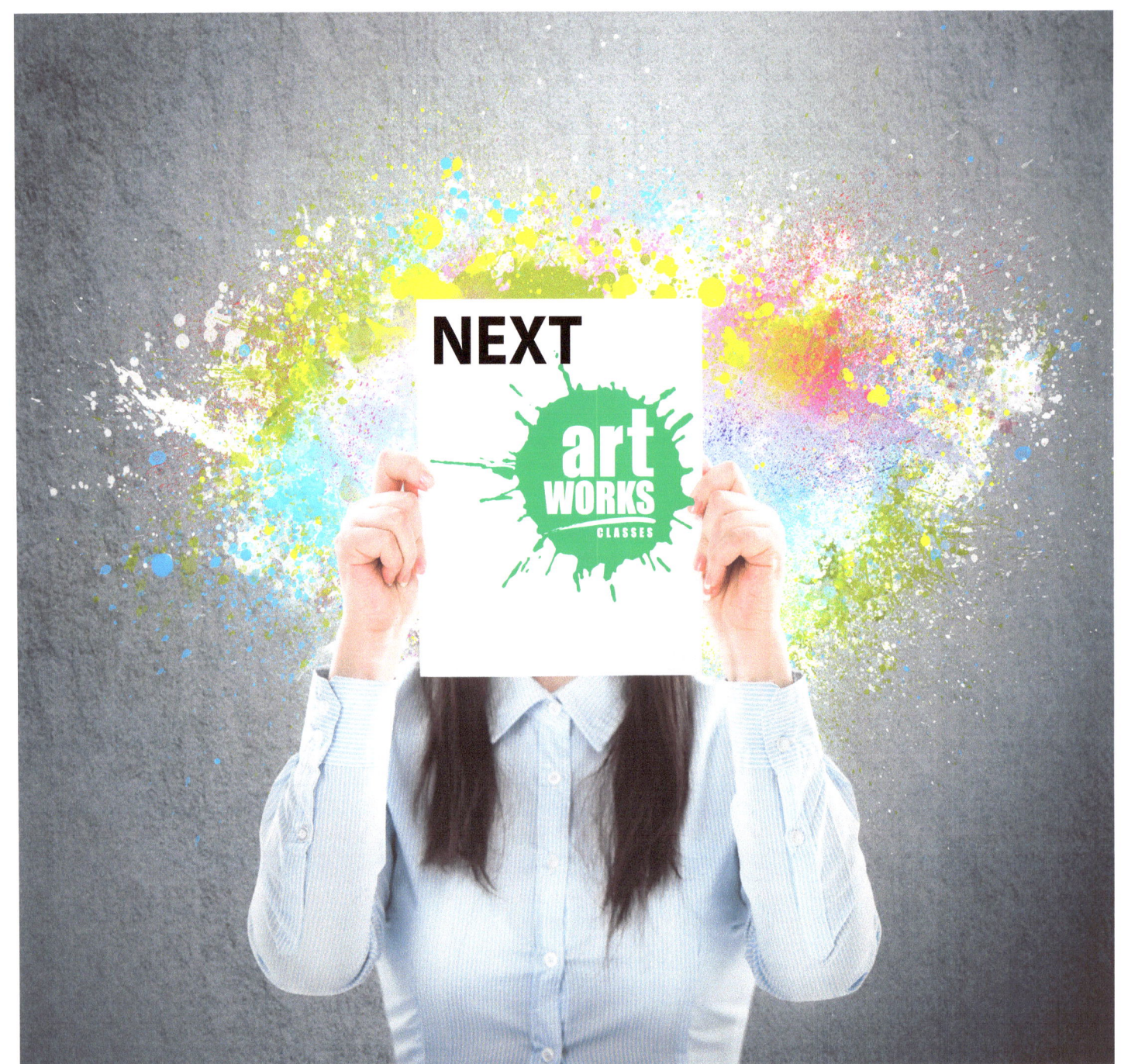

Locations

Bethesda MD
301 656 0044
bethesda@artworksclasses.com

McLean VA
703 288 9008
mclean@artworksclasses.com

www.artworksclasses.com